MattieBreathes

Tracie Loux

Mattie Breathes

photography by Dorean Beattie

Hi, I'm Mattie. I like music and making lots of noise with my favorite instrument, my
maraca. My favorite cartoon is Mickey Mouse Clubhouse. I like playing with my
brothers and sisters. They're helping me learn sign language too. They're super cool!

My dad and mom have helped me through a lot of hard stuff, and tvvhey've always
been by my side. I spent the first eleven months of my life in a hospital. For a long
time, they told me about this place called "home." They told me it was awesome.
When I finally got to go there, guess what I found out? They were RIGHT!

Dad and Mom tell me that I'm a joy giver. Well, I sure do love people, and it seems
like it's never too hard for me to make new friends smile.

This is my family. They love me a lot. The cool kids in this book that help me tell my story are my siblings, Aiden, Emma, and Elia.

(from left to right)
Elia, Nicholas, Isabelle, Aiden, Daddy, Mommy, Taylor, and Emma

If you want to learn more about our lives you can visit my mom's blog, "From the Heart." She writes lots of cool stories about us. You can find it at www.tracieloux. wordpress.com. If you would like to write us a note, you can email us at mattiebreathes@gmail.com.

What others have to say about
MattieBreathes

"'Mattie Breathes' ... A powerful and beautifully written educational book. Contained within, there is the most sincere and raw emotion only a loving mother could convey."

-Winston M. Manimtim, MD

"Making complex concepts accessible to everyone is a challenge faced by medical personnel and parents on a daily basis. "Mattie Breathes" does a great job of taking away fear of the unknown and adding the peace and security that understanding brings."

-Bethany Chu (Sign Language Interpreter and Mom to Trach-Hero, Penny)

"As a nurse practitioner who works with infants, I am pleased to have a book that I can recommend to families when facing the decision regarding a trach. I have cared for many patients and families before, during, and after this decision process. The actual photographs of this book bring a real life dimension that is missing in many references. This book presents the reality of life with a trach, as well as the truth that having a trach does not mean that someone cannot fully enjoy life. Kudos to Tracie and her team for tackling this worthy project."

- Jillane H Downs, RNC, MS, NNP-BC

"This children's book is a great educational resource for families of children who have tracheostomies. The main character is precious, the pictures are adorable, and the storyline makes the scary idea of a tracheostomy more understandable for children. It is definitely a great buy!"

-Callie Henderson, RRT-NPS

"I know that facing the decision of having your child receive a tracheostomy is a big, scary step for
parents. In my experience, with the right training and preparation, this can be a huge step forward for growth, healing, and development for many children. They have fewer hospitalizations, enabling them to spend more time at home bonding with their families. This family has been an inspiration and a great
resource for families facing this decision, and this book will be an awesome tool for these families as well!"

-Kimberly Lucas, RRT

"Mattie Breathes is by far the best book on children with trachs who need ventilator support. As a mommy of a child with special needs, I had to make the choice for my child to have a tracheostomy and be placed on a ventilator when she was 4 months old. I wish this book had been in my hands then to let me know that trachs and ventilators were not as scary as I had thought. Bravo to Tracie Mickey Loux for writing this book to help us all to understand and not fear trachs and ventilators."

-Shelley Colquitt, (Freelance Writer at Complex Child E-Magazine, and Mom to Trach-Hero, Zoe)

Mattie-what a little ray of sunshine! With a family by his side who believes in his ability to have utter joy in his life despite some minor 'glitches'. This little book can help replace fear with the conviction that life must sometimes be supported in very intricate ways. It gently guides the reader through the process of choosing a trach to help even the smallest child to breathe deeply and to grow. This will surely help family and friends to understand this seemingly complex process and to know that underneath it all, Mattie is just a little boy who wants to have fun!

Linda Risley, APRN

This book is dedicated to the hundreds of children who have prayed for Mattie and shared in his journey.

Put your hand on your chest and take a deep breath.

Did you feel that?

Just underneath your hand are your lungs (lŭngs). Your lungs help fill your body with air, called oxygen (ŏk-sĭ-jĕn). And your heart pumps good blood filled with oxygen to your body.

This helps you live and be strong.

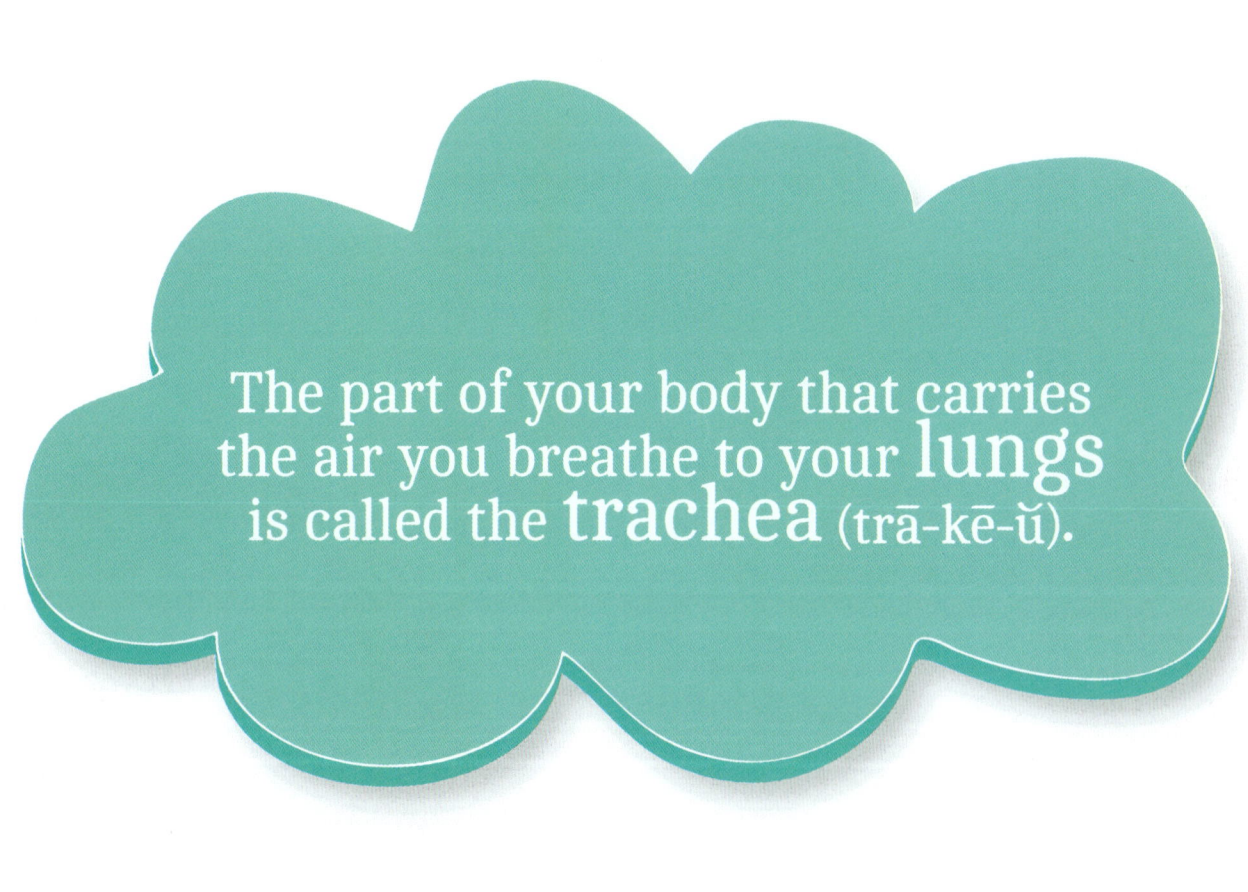

The part of your body that carries the air you breathe to your **lungs** is called the **trachea** (trā-kē-ŭ).

Mattie's **lungs** got hurt when he was a baby.

You know how you get a cold and it's hard to breathe through your nose?

Well, Mattie got so sick that it was very hard for air to get through his **trachea** and into his **lungs**.

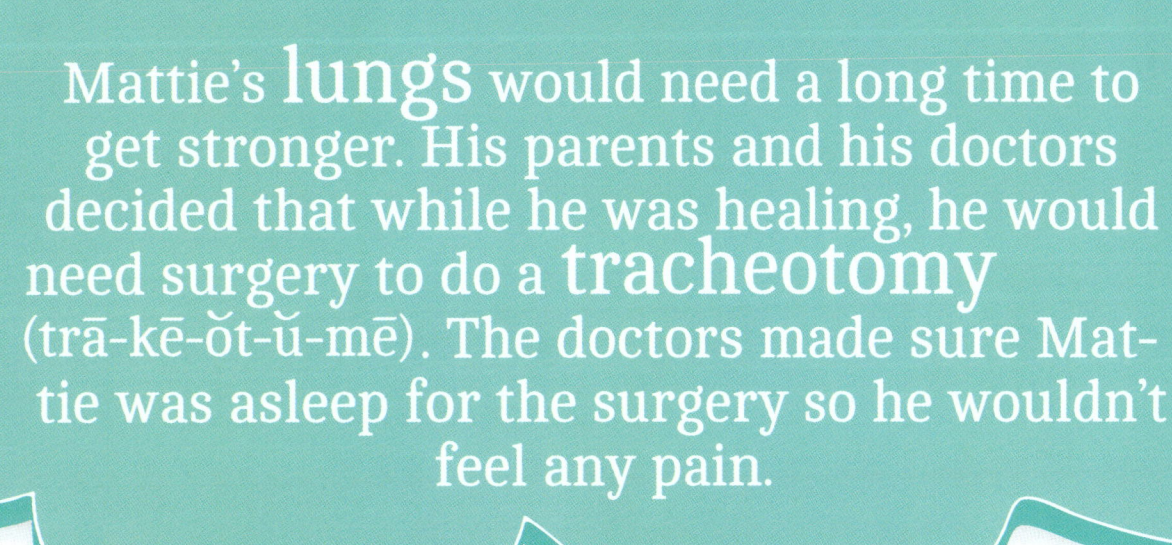

Mattie's **lungs** would need a long time to get stronger. His parents and his doctors decided that while he was healing, he would need surgery to do a **tracheotomy** (trā-kē-ŏt-ŭ-mē). The doctors made sure Mattie was asleep for the surgery so he wouldn't feel any pain.

Put your finger on your throat. Draw a line to the bottom where you feel a little dip.

A **tracheostomy** (trā-kē-ŏs-tŭ-mē) is the spot where the doctors made a hole for Mattie to breathe. This hole, a **stoma** (stō-mŭ), creates an airway. In order to keep this airway open, the doctor put in a short tube called a **trach** (trāk). Special ties wrap around Mattie's neck to hold the **trach** in place.

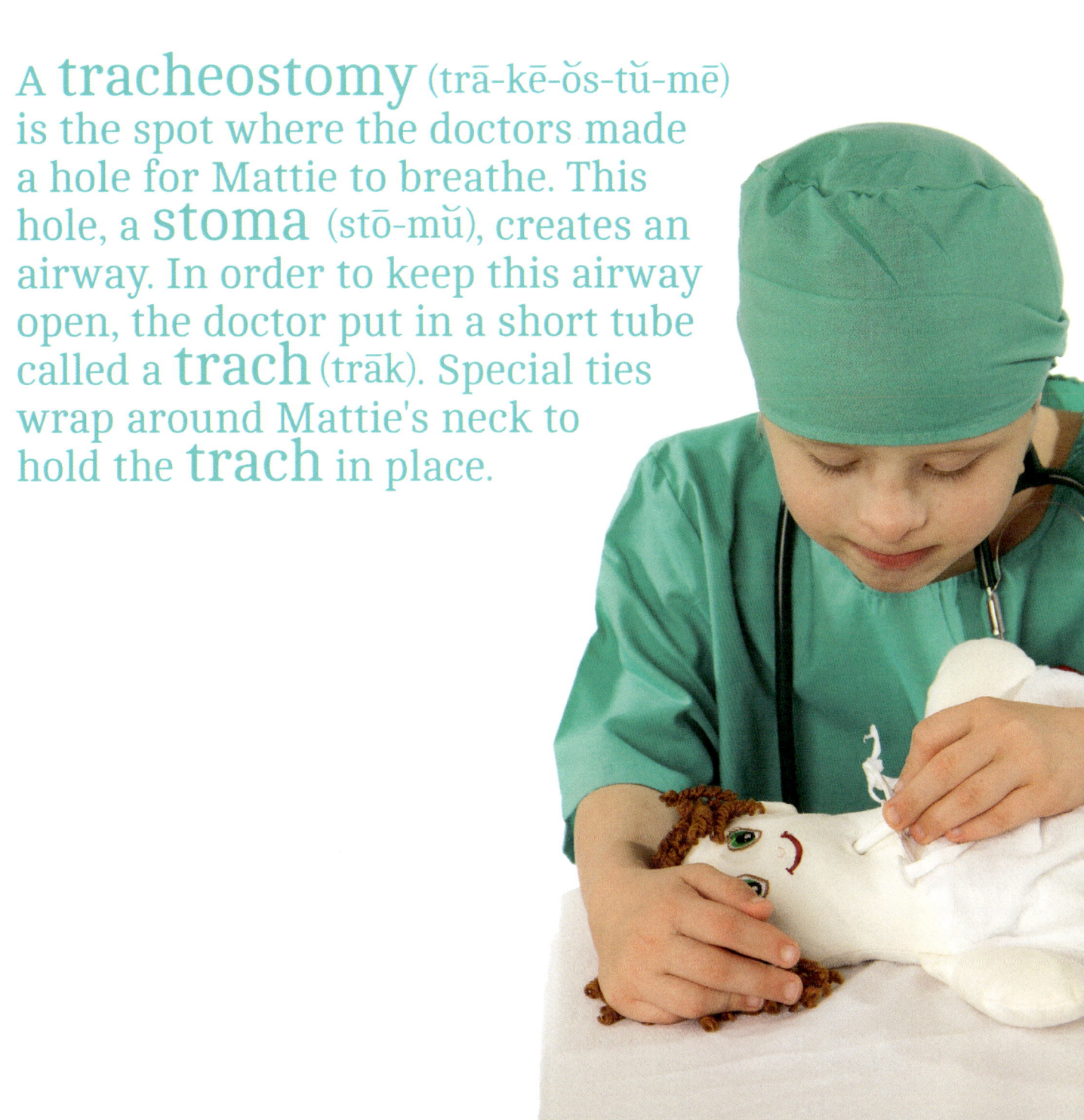

When you breathe in, you take great big breaths sometimes.

When you play hard and run, you take lots of little breaths to get good air into your lungs.

Take a minute and practice. Take a few BIG deep breaths. Now take a few short, fast breaths.

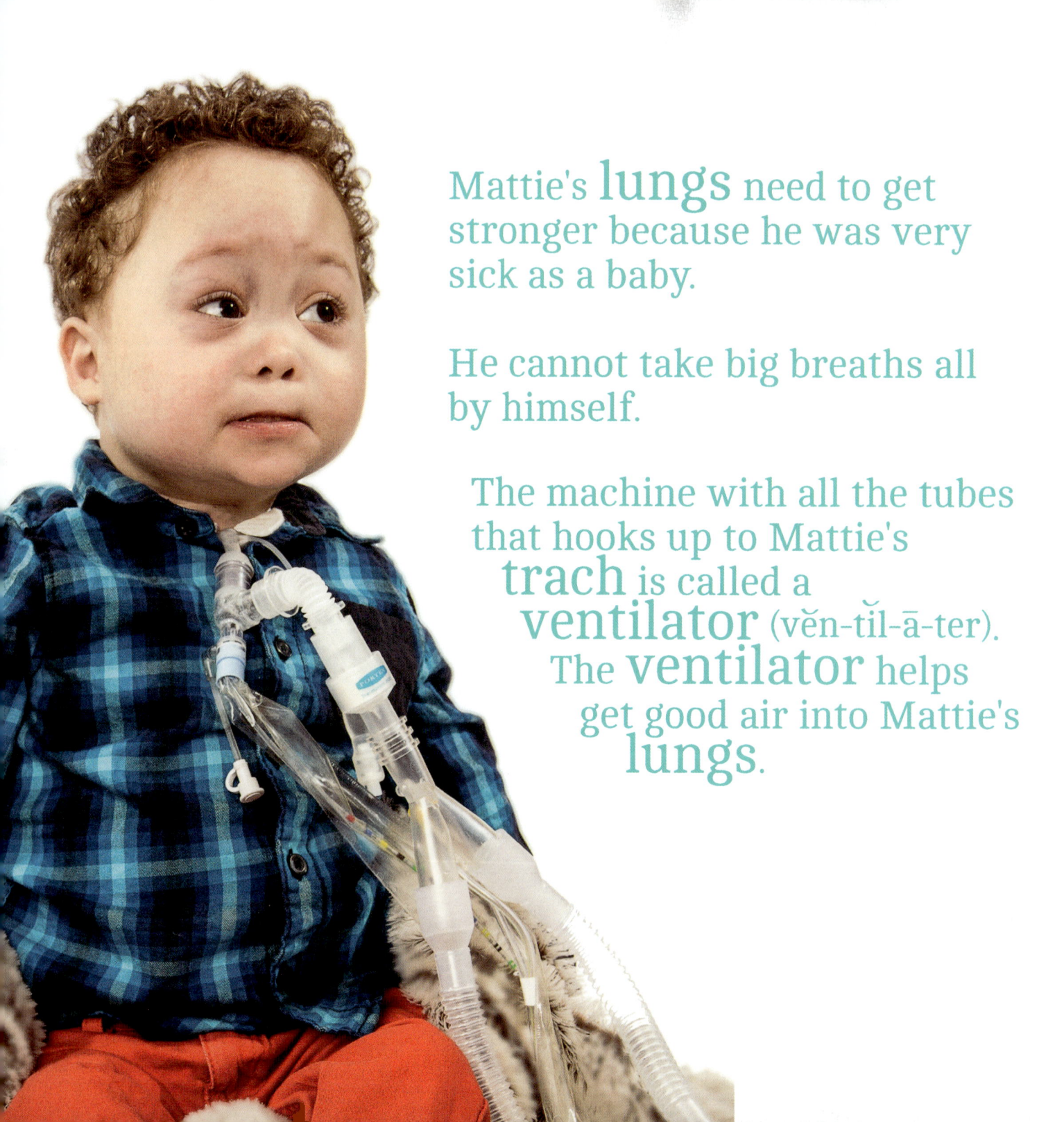

Mattie's **lungs** need to get stronger because he was very sick as a baby.

He cannot take big breaths all by himself.

The machine with all the tubes that hooks up to Mattie's **trach** is called a **ventilator** (vĕn-tĭl-ā-ter). The **ventilator** helps get good air into Mattie's **lungs**.

Some children with a **tracheostomy** also need the help of a **ventilator** for breathing.

Airway Pressure (cmH₂O)

-10   0   10   20   30   40   50   60   70   80   90   100

Controls

Breath Rate
bpm

Tidal Volume
ml

Pres. Control
cmH₂O

Insp. Time
sec

Pres. Support
cmH₂O

Sensitivity
lpm

Alarms

High Pres. Limit
cmH₂O

On/Standby

Volume   Pressure

Asist/Ctrl   SIMV/CPAP

Manual Breath

Control Lock

Set Value

Select   NPPV   Select

When Mattie takes his breaths, he breathes as big as he can. Sometimes it's not quite big enough. The ventilator helps him and blows a little extra air into his lungs to help him get a good, strong breath.

Sometimes, when Mattie gets very tired, he might even forget to take some of the breaths that he needs. So, the machine takes those breaths for him.

Do you remember when you were little? You needed to hold your mommy or daddy's hand to help you walk because your legs weren't quite strong enough.

You grew and got stronger. You didn't need help anymore. You could walk all by yourself.

It's the same with Mattie. Mattie needs help when he breathes. As he gets bigger, he won't need as much help. Someday, he will be big enough and strong enough to breathe without help.

But for now, Mattie has help to breathe.

Aren't you glad?

Because he can laugh.

And sing.

And play.

And Mattie is very, very happy.

List of Terms

Trachea (trā-kē-ŭ) Wind pipe.

Tracheostomy Tube (trā-kē-ŏs-tŭ-mē tūb) A tube that is inserted into the opening of the trachea to keep the airway open.

Trach (trāk) Short for tracheostomy tube.

Tracheostomy (trā-kē-ŏs-tŭ-mē) The opening into the trachea.

Tracheotomy (trā-kē-ŏt-ŭ-mē) A medical procedure creating an opening in the trachea.

Stoma (stō-mŭ) An artificial opening in the body created by surgery.

Oxygen (ŏk-sĭ-jĕn) One of the main elements that makes up the air. It is needed for survival.

Lungs (lŭngs) The organ in our body that exchanges carbon dioxide from the blood with the oxygen that we breathe.

Ventilator (vĕn-tĭl-ā-ter) A machine that helps a person breathe.

Dear Medical Professionals and Educators,

I'm just a mom who loves her kid. I remember the day I had to make the final decision on my college major. I had vacillated between the medical field and education. I decided to become an educator, never knowing that one day I would earn my medical degree at the "School of Hard Knocks." I'm part respiratory therapist, part nurse, and often "Doctor Mom."

When my husband and I, along with our amazing medical team, made the decision to have our son receive a tracheostomy, we discovered that there were very few resources available for us to explain this to our children and other family members.

It is my hope that this book will be placed in the hands of many families, to aid them in communicating with their children, extended family members, friends, neighbors, and even their child's classmates.

I encourage you to make this book available to your patients and their families. We hope that in sharing our story, other families will be encouraged and gain strength and hope for their own child's bright future.

Parent to Parent,

When our son Mattie was born in the fall of 2010, we had no idea what the months to follow would bring. We knew he had Down syndrome, and shortly after he was born we were told that he had a major heart defect that would require surgical correction. Never did we dream that in February of 2011, we would be faced with one of the hardest decisions of our lives.

After months of watching our son struggle to breathe, the medical team caring for him began to discuss with us the possibility of Mattie getting a tracheostomy. I remember not wanting to hear about it. I remember feeling so overwhelmed and scared. But I immediately thought of a dear friend whose child was living with a tracheostomy, and I contacted her. I don't remember much of what she said, but I do remember this. She said, "Tracie, you're doing this FOR him, not TO him."

After much discussion, we did decide that a tracheostomy was the very best thing for our son. We wanted him to live life to the fullest, to experience home and family, and we knew that without a trachoestomy, he would just get sicker and sicker. We knew that without a tracheostomy, he might die.

If this book is in your hands, you are either facing this same decision, or you have walked it out with your own child. I want you to know that you are braver and stronger than you think you are. You can do this. You may be afraid, but you will learn and grow in ways you never imagined.

I remember seeing our son after his tracheostomy, breathing with ease. His color was better, and he was able to grow and heal. He eventually became strong enough to have two much needed heart surgeries. And finally, he was able to come home and join his family.

It is my hope that this book will help you to see the joy and fullness of life that can come to your child. I hope that what you see in the pages of this book is a child who is loving life, enjoying being part of a family, and who is able to grow and experience life to the fullest.

As I have reminded myself many times on this journey, I encourage you as parents,

Don't Forget to Breathe

Commonly Asked Questions

Will a trach hurt my child? A properly inserted trach will not hurt. Your child will be able to move about and play and enjoy life without pain.

Will my child be able to eat by mouth? A child with a trach can still eat. Your medical team will help you know when your child is ready for this and if any special accommodations need to be made.

Will my child need a tracheostomy forever? Not all children need a tracheostomy forever. You will need to discuss this with your medical team. They can more fully predict your child's longterm prognosis. Many children simply need time for their lungs to grow and heal.

What if my child is playing and the trach gets pulled out? This can seem scary at first, but you will be trained by your medical team and before you know it, you will be able to replace a trach with ease.

Is taking care of a child with a tracheostomy a lot of work? Taking care of a child with a tracheostomy is definitely a bit more challenging than changing diapers, feeding, and bathing. There are many things you will have to learn, but you will be well prepared before you leave the hospital. You will most likely also qualify for home nursing support. You will also have a medical team at your service to answer your questions at any time. You will not be alone.

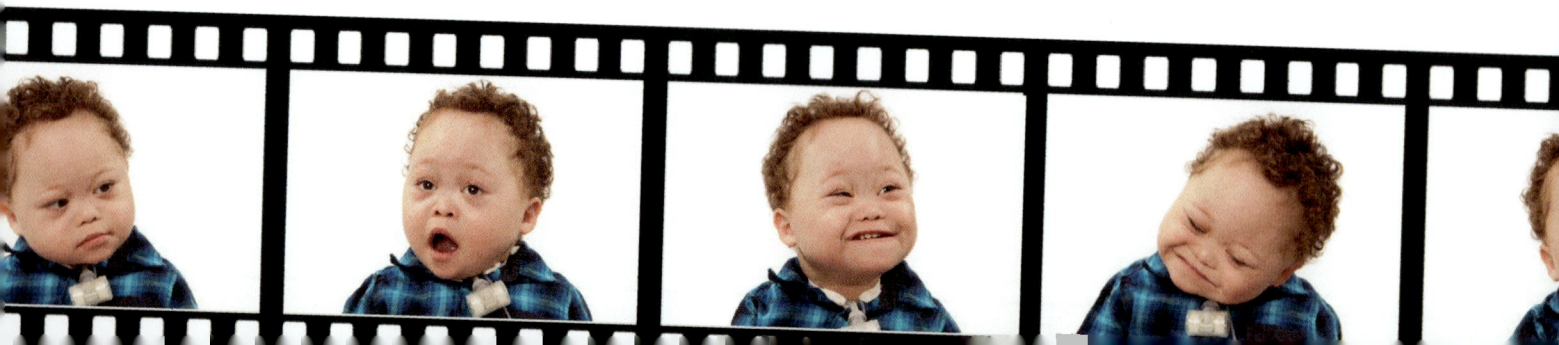

Will my child be able to talk?
A child with a tracheostomy can often eventually make noise. At first however, it is more than likely that your child will lose their voice. This was a hard thing to get used to. It's sad to watch your child cry without hearing them. Eventually as your child grows and gets stronger, it may be possible for them to "talk" around their trach, and at some point wear a special valve called a Passy Muir Valve that enables them to talk.

Does every child with a tracheostomy need a ventilator?
No, based on the respiratory needs of each child, sometimes all a child needs is a clear, open airway to be able to breathe with ease. Other children have lung damage or other difficulties that require the aid of a ventilator.

What machines will my child have?
Your child will have a suction machine to help clear his/her airway of mucus. Your child will have an oximeter to help monitor their heart rate and breathing rate. Many children also require an apnea monitor to further monitor their heart and breathing rates. Some children require the support of oxygen. You may have oxygen tanks and/or an oxygen concentrator in your home. You will be well-trained on all of this equipment.

How in the world will my child be able to get around with all of that gear?
Your child can be fitted with a special chair that can accommodate his/her medical equipment. At home, your child can learn to roll, sit, crawl, and walk in spite of all this equipment. You may be busy untangling from time to time, but you'll be surprised how little your child will be hindered.

Printed in Great Britain
by Amazon